Stations of the Lost

STATIONS OF THE LOST

Brian Wickers

Mansfield Press

Printed in Canada

Library and Archives Canada Cataloguing in Publication

Wickers, Brian, 1964-
Stations of the lost / Brian Wickers.

Poems.
ISBN 1-894469-28-3

I. Title.

PS8645.I25S68 2006 C811'.6 C2006-904597-6

Design: Mansfield Creative
Cover Photo: iStockphoto

The author would like to thank the editors of the following publications where many of these poems first appeared: Poetry; Literary Review of Canada; The New Quarterly; The Paris Review; The Atlantic Monthly; Prairie Fire; Descant; The Malahat Review. The author also gratefully acknowledges the support of the Canada Council for the Arts, the Ontario Arts Council and the Manitoba Arts Council.

A special thank you to:
Bill, Jim, George, Melissa, Mark, Veralyn, Steve, Mom, Liane, Gloria, David, Dale, Harold, Paula, Margaret, Jake, Molly, and Denis.

The publication of *Stations of the Lost* has been generously supported by the Canada Council for the Arts and the Ontario Arts Council.

The Canada Council for the Arts since 1957 | Le Conseil des Arts du Canada depuis 1957

Ontario Arts Council
Conseil des Arts de l'Ontario

Mansfield Press Inc.
25 Mansfield Avenue, Toronto, Ontario, Canada M6J 2A9
Publisher: Denis De Klerck
www.mansfieldpress.net

Table of Contents

True to Life

Account

We'd feared it since the first hints,
the fingers tightening into a fist.

And when we sat him down and gently
asked him to count back

from twenty, we never meant it
to be a countdown –

there should be plenty
of time for that. It was a litmus

for dementia or Alzheimer's.
I never meant it

to be mean, either, though it must
have been humbling when I set the timer

and he stumbled
through the largest seven numbers – teen

years, the age when almost everything
was on the edge of happening. He paused

around twelve or eleven, resumed
at six, but in that panicked, odd

span of missing years, got to his feet and
walked out of the living room. Bliss

lit his face in the next, like he'd been
listening to music – oblivious

to our vexed attentions.
Then it was obvious

even to us
that dad was getting on

with his life
by getting over it.

Don't Go Back

Because it will be perfect,
eaves weighed down with leaves
now fixed, a new cedar deck,

no doubt paid for. A surface
paved and slick
where your wreck of a car

once rested. A garden
where the derelict
lilacs dripped, neat

and weeded. A backyard
where so little care
after all was needed.

And in spite of the drizzle
no defeated, dismal air.
Don't go back because the street

mistrusts such visits;
because to stand in the cold
mist and admit its hold

is outlandish. Because its shadow
was cast years ago.
Because when you're driven past

the house you once lived in
you might light on a child
lost in a game. If it's given

that he's your double
let's give him
glasses to catch

how the world will outlast him
until that troubled
feeling passes –

and a failing smile
while he sees how foreign
seem those lives before him,

or the end of these days
when met by a rain.
And because when it does

rain again and again
it does for them, in a way
that won't be explained.

Overheard

All that week he wouldn't speak.
And when we wheeled him there
and tucked him in, he turned his face
to the wall, as though we were already
dead to him, or he were already
barely in his body.

That rush of air – all hushed
and warm – that seems as enormous
as love must in such a place,
eddied when, turning over in bed, she
said, are you ready
now to talk to me?

Oversight

Would someone, please, come forward
for the boy who found his way

from the crowd to the Lost
and Found? He is sorry for misbehaving –

and grateful, of course,
care is being taken

to find his parents, now that he's been seen
waiting with patience. He'd been crying,

once – scared when it crossed
his mind he might have

to stay awhile – but has staved off
the ache of it, and is trying

to sit with a smile
in the special chair,

where he is being brave
for his parents' sake.

He has been waiting with some patients
in the care ward, where the waiting can take

the day, or years. He is keeping careful
watch on the way the tiles appear

to scatter the aisle. No more apparent –
that pattern – than how it breaks

against his chair into voices
clearly beyond him. He is never alone,

though he sits still and is rarely fitful
or prone to wander. And though

he tends instead to nod and wake
or stares, mistaking noises, we know

he is aware he has something
he has been trying

to get out of his mind. So long
as he can say it. So long

as you can make it out
for him, confined

by words these days.
If you've heard,

you can find your way
home to him.

Stranded

We know where we left you
for the best,

in a home meant
for the rest

of your days,
but not exactly where we lost you,

or you lost your way.
I elect the moment

I held your hand and said, let's go,
when instead of a button you pressed

a metal eyelet
on the door of the elevator –

and then we were stranded on an island
freighter at night and frightened

that no one was headed home. Later,
I let go,

I said, of the past
but when pressed

to find you in some lost
childhood time, I could not help

but head back
here instead, to the last

of us, as though that were as far
as I could go. And far enough.

Modelling To Scale

For model railroaders there is no detail
too trivial to the trained eye: precisionists,
they count rivets, can't live with improper-sized rail
for sidings and mainlines, envision this
rudimentary private paradise
of dusty farmland, trees, and harmless industry.
But not today: like someone had rolled a pair of dice,
and just as he'd feared, his favourite model tree,
the ornamental maple, tore out
a station made from scratch, felled by his own arm.
Every loss is real. But at his age, tears count
for less. You lose track. And who's left to quiet?
Crying like nothing from the friendly giant
could ever come to harm.

Overview

Back home on vacation, he'd been milling around
the downtown's mostly vacant ghostmall, milking –
was it loss, nostalgia? Stopping to recall which stalls
were gone, which still the same – that comical, grim
game of survival and change, like his own, a puzzled
tourist in the archive of past lives, or a pilgrim
relishing the relic to feel some sense of blame
relinquished. But also just to visit his favourite store.
Its intricate model kits and showcase window, trimmed
with scale trains and sylvan villages, became a whole
other world, laid on a table. Tranquil, stable,
though it must have been at such a cost
unavailable to him – much as he'd loved being lost
in that landscape of simple imagination.
But when he came upon the very same
spot, he remembered again when he'd found it
closed up long ago. So it vanished all over. A second time
a child, something stilled in him, astounded
that he'd forgotten – how? why? – to recognize
the space that replaced it. He felt severed,
estranged, and not from some changing nuance
of nostalgia but from the here and now. What he knew once
more, friends elsewhere or moving on, was like a feeling
failing to deepen into something new, like someone's clever
way of showing you for good and forever you can keep
losing what wasn't ever yours.

Stations Of The Lost

The two-story fence of the nuns' reformatory
not meant as a prison, it was often mentioned.
The riverbank's visionary far shore we
imagined a country of another time. The mansions
and gardens of the crescent we regarded as foreign
and our own. And the rails, a scar the park had forgiven,
rusting into the enormous green graveyard of the abandoned
embankment above us, ending abruptly
where the trestle used to be, and where chain links informed us
that travel was trespass and distance forbidden,
though at every random whistle I ran to meet an engine.
These borders so defined me by the age of seven
that when I go back it is to find them again
but always as the boy who had gone
far too far beyond them one day

to believe he belonged. It is an early fall. That rain
of leaves falters when the wind halts. When the chain came off
his bicycle, everything changed. It was no one's fault,
but he feels he is to blame; he will have to wheel it home.
The distance seems terrible. Home is no longer the same.
Opened eyes notice all he had missed, flashing past.
The rails of a trolley line, cracked through the asphalt.
The distant brewery stacks behind the church spires, the path
trespassing the grounds of Our Holy Saviour, to the fence
and through a gracious ancient graveyard. An impression
of being followed pursues him. It feels like he has been
given a question whose answer is false; he has some sense
already of how small and precarious his place is –
that space he's been banished from. He is abashed and
ashamed; every landmark he passes, he imagines
vanishing after him.

Early Housing

Back in the community tracts,
we grew up making the crudest things of beauty
from those humble building blocks of Lego,
then decreed them crumbling wrecks, ready
to be smashed. Rudimentary bungalows
to century homes we made our practise.
My older brother holds me back, bridling to let go,
and I blunder out of the blocks, my heart gone
into a song of praise or wonder at breaking
my own record as apprentice homewrecker,
though something almost from the get go
inside said, prosaically, this was wrong, wrong,
while impressive billows of pretend dust settled.
I'll say, if you're taking this as some unsubtle
way of placing blame, please understand
I knew better. We were complicit – in it together.
After I'm stopped, I'm looking up, a bit stunned
by the appearance of my parents, their feather-
light laughter, while over us an odour like tar extends
from a flashbulb dark as asphalt in father's hand.

Candor

The first moment that I remember having spoken,
at least, what I'd recall of it, became an emblem
of my less than candid relations with the family – and
ironical because it happened just before I ran from all
of them. I am standing still in the token panorama,
refusing – see the crossed arms? – to have my picture taken
framed on the step of my brother's brand new tricycle,
as Steven got to sit, grinning like a villain behind his handlebars,
and, beside him, Dad was fiddling sadly with the camera,
while Mom was somehow out of sight. I must have seen stars
that moment, felt something fickle in Dad's wishes –
or maybe to refuse was all that I could do or say.
But it sometimes seems I'd stopped because an anguish
for which I'll never find the proper language
began in me then, and grew. Suddenly I'd a mind to move away.
Ever since, I've dreaded heading in the same direction.
As for what happens afterwards, I suppose I never really knew,

there being no competing points of view to go on.
With one exception, to be honest. I have this photo,
black and white, and perfectly in focus. I'm astonished, posed
with Steven on his trike, without a trace of conflict on my face.

The Separation

From where I sat in the stairwell –
the age of twelve – I began to see how the scene
was changing into a sort of farewell
more important, then, than for what it would mean.
Mom held herself, rocking, and said she felt ill.
The clock ticked on because all talk had ceased.
Gripping the railing I stared through, I fell still.
Then Dad was yelling into the receiver,
calling for Children's Aid to come;
Steven had pounded the walls last evening.
From holding on so tight, my hand went numb.
Couldn't they see what was going to happen?
Now that the clock was pounding I saw myself
writing a letter – one telling enough, or else
one to warn them how this had to end. How apt, then,
my trying to keep us pieced together
by writing it out, as I do, now, here.
And how clearly the matter was settled
as I sat there, with the letter
composing itself over the years.

Elevation

The venerable professor,
out on a limb on a broadcast,
spoke of how the angels were with us
once again. How odd that
they've come back so diminished,
absent save as agents
of our vainer and lesser
wishes. Then he listed
over the radio
their replacements: the auras,
the gems and crystals,
the magic strategems of the New Age's
bent, seeking to fix at a whim
that unsteady ratio
between the weight of our hearts
and the head of a pin.
The chorus of mixed feelings before us!
The indifferent
day that you drifted out of my life, love,
and slipped and fell
on the landing of the exit,
as your cloak swept up
to save yourself, I saw
an angel's opening wings in it,
for maybe the balance
of that anomalous
second or so when my heart went out
like a candle, and my breath
made you a halo.
But none of us,
I had to tell myself,
could bear up under such
weighty comparison.
It brought me back at once

to the delicate morning I held
my lightening head in my hands,
weighing word
of a brother in a hospital ward,
against that of my dad,
ready to land
in the other wing,
while I sat on a bathroom floor,
saying *take him*
or praying the same.

The Bargain

Coming across one in some Second Hand,
with the former owner's name sewn
over a more desirable label, I'm forced
back to my dad's green merino argyle,
for which I paid more than he could afford
and made a salesclerk fuss for quite a while
undressing dad's size from the mannequin.
The Home's dryers were shrinking anything
they were wearing thin. Before I knew better
why I'd tried to refashion him
in the image of his English accent, the sweater
was looking like it was wearing him
down. What I hadn't bargained for: his smile
tighter, uncertain, and the skin waxen.

Sometime

After his eyes, vacant
skies, gave up speaking
for dad, something unspoken

someone had awakened
in him grew into a grief
or a regret

he couldn't keep
a secret. So he kept
himself by a window,

and when we came closer
said, I had to end it
over and over

to the pane, then ended
our little visit
by looking back again,

then as now – is it
at the sky? – as if
looking at someone.

A sky as if
someone once
imagined it.

An Aesthetic

Years ago, when Mom could no longer bear
some money burden – and forbidden to work –
she turned for advice to her mother. Who turned chary
with words: get rid of the pet. Mom kept that hidden
for years on her mother's imaginary headstone.

Yet here we are driving again to the vet.
I've been telling her how it's all for the best.
They can't afford to let the new apartment go,
though the complex won't allow them pets.
And as for Dad, you know...

Dad will never know. She held on to Sam
with a towel. A hazel-eyed Maine Coon, supple
and muscled, with a greying muzzle. He howled.
Had we come too soon – Sam, son,
Mom and absent husband? I was puzzled

how heavy he'd become, whatever he became
when the needle went in. And the feelings drained
until everything seemed lighter again.
Turning to hand her the folded towel
I suddenly needed to know

how she'd made it so far
to the door of the car, in tears. At supper
she set her cup down and told her story
of her mother. To think that, before,
we'd sat in that car like a couple

of strangers. As though now we know better
who we were. Or are. Before we cried for Sam,
for her, and maybe for husband,
I tried to look hard
at my hands, for blood or for scars.

Second Hand

When I bent to touch the oversize collar
on their brittle, fenced-in terrier
he astounded me, sinking his trembling
fangs between my thumb and index finger,
tearing a fleshy round there. Scars appear once
I flex my hands, which more and more are resembling
the slender pair of my long buried father.

By the time I rushed home to my parents, I'd figured
that I wasn't after justice, just some comfort
but dad had insisted. Putting on his pale blue jacket
he drew me after him. And when he shook his fist
at no one over the fence, it looked frail and
insignificant, the wrist caught in an elastic cuff.

Was that all I'd arrived at, that no one is perfect?
I knew he'd threaten to throw me in there, to toughen me up,
the way his dad had made him fit, those helpless seconds,
to sink or swim. Was I fast enough to think
that if I could pity him, the madness might pass
in me as wisdom? And that I'd pity myself less, sickened
by an inkling that nothing was fixed, and everything
was going to stay that way?

Ring

She's been minding his bedding and
finds her husband's wedding band
has slipped from his finger
to wind up in the folds.
The warmth it holds lingers
and the old gold fascinates.
The poor nurse looks aghast
and, worse, offers to fasten it
while he lies like a ghost.
She feels the ring going cold,
but needs something to clutch
when she touches that hand
to make him wake up
as much as he can. Touch strands
of hair and his hospital band
as keepsakes or tokens.
She has taken so much,
knowing more must be taken.
The ring she'll keep and place
close as her chest or closet,
in an act of remembrance
she will have to embrace.

Ronald Seymour, Winnipeg Yards, Station Overpass

Watching the train assembled below
into the Transcontinental's steelgold,
did my dad remember his journey
here, one he carried like an injury
to his pride? The prairie-wide sky still holds
in such memories. And I know it is in
the what-might-have-been that this citizen
of elsewhere lived his life, looking half natural
in his British brogues, with hat and satchel,
hating when he had to hop the daily freight
and table the waybill. I couldn't wait,
at nine, to head behind his wooden gait.
Already I understood him
on a hunch as a figure of pathos
but felt in my father's losses a loss
more general, as though it also belonged
almost anywhere else – where he still longed
to be. Early in the last century
he entered as landed gentry,
eager to give all he had to offer,
table manners, tales of an Officer:
tennis matches with the Heir Apparent,
or Presumptive, rather. My poor father.
Enigmatic, absent-minded parent
from whom we learned never to bother
asking for real detail. After the War went
so very wrong for him, these weren't
hints of station enough to warrant
even a modest placement home.
And then what place meant Home?

He'd been as sure of his future
as his past, when so few were.
But when you can't put the two

together, what can you do?
If you were my father,
you'd have hunched your shoulders
against the cold, and folded under
your arm the morning newspaper,
shouldering the world as new-world pauper.
Mister Ronald Seymour,
soldier of phlegmatic demeanor
and seldom the kind or mean word:
mystic, mannered, ascetic, and minor
spy in the War, your mystique
proved stronger than your mistakes
for me, having come at least this far
above the yards, climbing despite a fear
of heights, meaning falling. Ronald Seymour,
I'd just as gladly have scattered
your ashes here, asking the gesture to matter,
meanwhile wishing you'd be more
than gestures I'd tried to master.
Try looking when the train leaves the rails
behind it; eyes shut, and the mind reels
back to the image of him leaving his village.
It has left for me the privilege
of hindsight, but seeing farther
the way a child believes he sees forever.
At least I'm child enough today to be amazed
that the mainline shining beyond this maze
of sidings and switches remains for some
a way out – or let's say one way onward,
and in this way I'll have honoured
both his pasts – his seeking
riches in the foreign and his eking
out a living here – knowing neither past
was wholly the path for him.

Travelling Distances

Dad, half way home and I'm still astonished
at the distance you've gone, waiting
out your age. I could never have wished
in my blackest rage for your gaunt
folds of skin, or shoulder blades as sharp
as angel wings, your translucent wrists, or the way
all the ends of your sentences have vanished
or finish elsewhere. I couldn't follow you,
though all through this early autumn slate
of leaf and evergreen you've haunted me. Grief
needn't wait, however we may need it –
later – to begin again.

I drive the shorter way home, north over Michigan's
orphaned forests, and through the mouth of the strait,
following shores, mists – the margins
of gulls mulling over breakers
and catching themselves short, calling out snatches
of that ancient song about reluctance, and aching
to belong, but above all about distance. Wish again
I could finish your thoughts. But the pine
forests are passing by so fast I decide
I could never have caught them anyhow,
while clouds fix in the watered-down sky
furious browlines. Was it only my curious face
you glimpsed as your phrases drifted away?
When the bridge lifts me over the lake
the window lets in briny gusts and the cries
of gulls calling in August. It's hard to listen
and harder yet to swallow. Far off, a wake
bears with me though my heart is still
so slow to follow.

Cargo

In a dark the shades have made
attentive, you can hear, beyond your breath,
brakes of the big rigs gearing down on the grade
and, below them for a minute, the sound of one
shuddering grain train, laden with cargo
bound for someplace you've never been yet.
You would think that driving into the sun
all day would put an end to that song
of longing, but even when gone we know
it can always come back, like now, larger
than life, to tell how it's been spent at dawn
in a motel bed three years after your death,
my mind elsewhere and my body gone
hard with misplaced ardour.

Evening

With sidewalk chalk or imagined missions
away and back on a bike, in ever-widening circles,
we took on the beckoning world
as our playing strayed into the evening.

Is it time to go in? A few crickets
whispering like music in the crisp air, a shiver,
and the late light thins, too quickly,
to silver or mother of pearl,

all things under a sky, that undiscovered country
of umber. Are you too far? Listen as voices begin
calling you back – loving, insistent,
but distant. You can still go in,

home to your bath and story and bed.
The lamplight's ample circle. So why in the world
are you standing instead,
waiting wet faced, and sorry?

Natural Life

Marginal Questions, Winter, English 101, Frost

Why does the speaker stop by the woods?
would you have stopped be honest
would you care to be in New England
breathing horses the evening forest
or elsewhere do you care for snow
at all are you still immortal
now that the snow is falling there
on the blank paper before us

Who owns the woods – in which of several senses?
do you own property have you ever tended to animals
would you own a wood if yes
are you dispossessed why are you all
bent over these desks
thinking of snow in the winter with
wind blowing snow past the windows

Why are the woods lovely and yet dark?
did you get an image was it vivid
could you help it
along maybe you felt alone welcomed overwhelmed
by nothing definite
enough you are so young and yet
how is this snow falling
like someone calling yes
not at all ominous

But I have promises to keep – why has he
decided to move on? what did he give up
did he hide it move on if you don't know
the deepening snow

And miles to go before I sleep – why else
might the sentence be repeated? ask yourselves
several if need be the second time did it
touch you the first time
did he touch the snow and go numb is he growing
weaker is the speaker dying or falling asleep
have you thought of either
or both
watching the snow falling from the snow
for years now here

and there why has it never come clear
whatever were you hoping for
all these weathers is it daunting
knowing the questions are endless
being tested you can be found wanting
questions without answers
what is your best guess
if you find your own will you nevertheless
let me know?

Pairs

I could never find the place
in my youthful way of seeing things
for the uncouth speed of the pair of nuns,
when their evening walking pace
rose to a run as they passed me, eyes on the path,
habits sweeping the pavement, and frowns unceasing
as the clouds on the horizon.
Not until the day an elderly nun
in a TV interview focused on how easily
the custody of the eyes might be broken
in the carefree act of glancing up,
tree-ward at birdsong, or at the laughter
beloved of St. Francis of Assisi.

It made sense of the couple of heartbeats after
my accidentally soaring frisbee
cleared the fence that kept on the grounds
the dangerous teenage girls, and landed
wholly out of bounds
in that school for wayward unwed women. Only eleven,
with a crush on every vaguely maternal person,
I noticed, but could not understand it
when the newly-wimpled novice looked away
at the same time that I did –
but how daring for her simply to stay there,
for one giddy, lovely, and candid
eye-opening moment, staring and beaming at me.

Pentimento

My humbling moment came at a remove, once
we were stationed before an Annunciation
with student wits, when one of mine, one of *those,*
hit upon the phrase the fricking Frick, and meant it
to be added to the mix. It echoed while we froze
in a room where the late light
met a lot of luminous, pent up gloom

and let it go. But I had had a moment
of illumination at The Met,
as those lovingly slow mouthed Os
in Bill Viola's still moving *Quintet*
of Remembrance began to awaken
in me, having vanished into the heart
of things missed – of everything after it's taken
so long so long to dawn and then depart.

A Seashell From The Seychelles

Sally by the seashore, letting the seadrift
sift through her half-closed fist, holds
not only an ear-shaped shell
of abalone, and relics of timber felled
from an age-old harvest of wreckage
to rest again in a skeletal forest,
but all the sea once held:
pearled eyes and coralled bone,
and the nautilus's whorled orifice,
risen from its ocean spell
to sit like a long-abandoned oracle,
but (listen) to sing from the still small
throne of its body...
                                        Lately,
my lady, so little abides
in the sound of those tides. Daily,
I've waited for your presence, for evidence, and found
the more the sea changes remains
into its own gains, the more I can explain
your silence. Let what's precious be
lost to most. At best, you are barely
fathomed in the shared depths
of a certain word. With hesitant steps,
I've waded into the sea's midst, hoping to see
merely your ghost. And what I've seen, turned shoreward
and to calm, seems more than
your boast. You've opened your palm.

Momentum

Now and then in fall the unsettled leaves
catch in those first dustings of snow, go molten,
and fall again, sinking into prints that match them,
opening their molds. I watch them gather. It happens
that I've seen leaves aloft cleaving together,
fine curled spines melting down as soft
as down to acrid loam, and smelt the scent
turn into incense as leaf musk rose. And though I've tried
to leave these stirrings alone, such a rich
mingling embodies a number of things
sinking in.
                    I'm thinking of them
as my thumb traces in the tip of your navel,
lips of a deliberate oval, and I wait
for the moment when your own lovely weight
comes on so slowly I could hardly know
the impression moving with me from something
deeper and more sudden. The pungent wet
they become, blackening on the lawn as the snow
cover's drawn back, could be the autumn
sleep given lovers. Oddly, it happens when their freed
bodies take everything in to freeze
the moment with them. Again as they come
another fall is ending, and the bough bends,
waiting for rain.

Sandman

That worker on a terrace
a little too close to our own

is putting a brave face
on this building's weathered brick,

paring off a surface
which bit after bit is weathering *us*,

its drift thickening, getting in
windows keyholes – we don't know

how and when we'll be rid of the grit
settling on skin, in hair, invading the bed.

Or when we'll awaken
to a morning free of the grating

irritating presence that has never, yet,
produced a pearl. But when

I smooth the deepening grain of your skin
as we begin

working a current that will carry us
into sleep – soon enough

the room becomes
mother-of-something.

Other-than-pearl.
Maybe a world.

The Still Life

Instead of waiting on edge for that painting
by Vermeer, or the spoken-for bones on a beach
to come clear off the page as an image
seldom-reached, I merely
held my breath

as five yellow finches set in relief
by their ruffled wet feathers worried the spider
inching through my own sideyard, and as Zuzu's quickening
retriever nostrils snuffled a pinecone until
the neighbour plucked his acoustic guitar –

and then I remembered that morning how far
I'd been carried, before I cared to ask
if the cascading yellowgreen rain forming a carpet,
I'm guessing, of maple seed casings,
was made of petal, husk, or even essence,

being such a mixed message, a blessing and artless.

Flower Catalogue

To soften the view and create a focus
the caption suggested a window framed by ficus
and a single hibiscus with its periscopic bloom:
often a few will more than do to fill a room.

But as soon as I saw one my preference was for us
to choose a delicate, purple and scarlet-skirted fuchsia
for its elegant bell and long-legged pistils. Then the sense
                                                            of déjà vu
began to end. Wafting from the catalogue, it left me at a loss

the gloss of my companion was to fill. She looked
                                                            until the beautiful
confusion was gone from her face: "they look
like captive ballerinas." And, like a hook, the idea
of seeing what I'd wanted took.

The Departure

Three in the morning and you've woken with your sleep
calling you to the brink of the deepening
wells around your eyes because a sound
rapid and quiet as water
in the sink or a mouse in the walls
of this broken down house has got her
out of bed again and crying to find in the silence
a part of her gone with him. Six months since
they've spoken, the diminishment
of a friendship that meant this much
by the end of it. And it isn't just
how it went, both of them waiting and out of touch,
but how it's way too late, you're thinking,
as you sink into the dream in which
you resemble him. So you switch
the light on, and it seems you're off
to find her somewhere in the dark out there,
if only to offer that token cup of water
because you have to care this much, in case,
in his wake, it seems you haven't enough –
and have you, if you haven't woken up?

Cloud Watch

Foreign terrain or an ocean, whole trains
of elephants, whales' tails, zephyrs, an ephemeral
iceberg or some effortlessly elegant
cipher – see, they're not so far

off as your thoughts. But neither are
they merely what they are – air,
light, and water, marine and emerald –
and rarely are you. Seldom

do we see ourselves in them.
Though we notice them, as we do stars,
in certain moods. Then they seem to start,
faster in memory, in dream sequences, where they frequent

skyscrapers, tenements, factories. They assume
shades of grey and elemental black and white,
beginning or ending the stories,
bringing on the night. They are moving

to a music lost to you
in childhood, in movement
lasting decades. Or a music understood
as nothing to do with

your past. They don't age,
but can change shape above a far place
and never arrive. They cross each other's paths,
going different speeds, billowing. They can look

the same after you've gone,
or appear out of nowhere, drawing nearer
as you stand there staring, saying, how eerie
that they're not alive. In a yellowing

luminous sky, they touch down chameleon
feelers, strange and dangerous. Or give off a fragrance
of spring or a mellowing
late rain. Ruminant above meadows, vagrant

over avenues – remember, they haven't any human
intentions, feelings, motives. We pass through them
mentioning cloud ceilings, as if they had many
rooms for us. They are best imagined

in a wind that drafts in a window.
Adrift for an instant until the magic
has ended, you blend in as they dwindle
into a too familiar distance.

Ars Poetica

Planting her feet instead to haul a Russian Olive back to shade,
the henna-tinted, suntanned gardener I'd instantly a crush on
shook her tresses and said, "you need to understand
                                        the apple blossom – "

nodding toward where trellised light and rapid cloud had made
whole rows of them into a dappling evanescence – "as seed
under stress, a survival mechanism. Those ones" –
                                        and her answer

came as sunlight happened to fade from her
face so palpably it hurt me – "those I've all but given up on.
They bloomed too early in the summer to live long."

Travels

Winnipeg, 1998

In the news all that week, scandals and sex...
The younger women gathered at my desk
in dresses, sandals, wonder exactly what I'm after, next
paper. A single hip brushing against the underlip
touches a sadness I can't address. My ex
calls about a date of departure. And that afternoon another
postcard from a friend, now in sunny Puerto Vallarta
on her honeymoon.
                                        "Although I'm married I can't say if
I feel any different. It is so beautiful
here. Write soon." Sometimes my heart and I want
to part company. On the dutiful
walk home from campus I come to where the oxbow
bends against the undertow, and am carried away with
a feeling I don't argue
is anything more than that melancholy echo,
calling as always *where are you?*

Church Going, St. Martin's Summer

Punctual as Sundays, if a little hazy past
the stained glass tinting on your windowpane,
they are making their way, some of them
making it last. The mainstays are the women,
still dressed in summer Sunday best,
complete with purses, and, sure enough,
gloves that match. Pursed lips.
The churches take each of them in
with love. You wait in your room.
Yet their willingness more than balances
the shortened services, the visitors' gruff
indifference except to rummage sales,
and others only curious about the wistful way
the summer-come-autumn light is playing
on the bell dome surrounding St. Martin of Tours
with a halo, right in front of your home.
From heathen to hermit, then, against his wishes,
to bishop, bound for heaven. His statue
has kept a certain attitude, though rumour has it
from time to time he may look back
at you. But today the autumn belongs
to these women. They even welcome in
that mumbling man – a wanderer by force of habit
back and forth across the street, and as stranded
as the stolid leaves he kicks at. May all of them keep
you settled into your windowseat, listening
for crickets, bells, and the christening click of heels;
lingering over your cigarette, coffee, and pocket novel
of broken romance and regrets. Where you wait
for the world to turn holy again. And then,
as luck would have it, lovers happen by.
From the other life you know, the one
you'd like to live, and haven't.

Hit And Miss

Zuzu's been in an accident, though exactly when
we'll never feel was fixed, beyond dispute.
She keeps her cinnamon tail tucked in, and refuses
to budge when traffic passes. She has invisible bruises
beneath the sheen of her crooked plume.
All of a sudden she wants to heel; we could never
train her to come. We'd lived too long in fear
of this not to feel wholly complicit,

and older. Watching her flanks shrink to a slip
we'd named her a Golden Retreater.
When she wouldn't fetch, a Golden Deceiver.
A Golden Nothing, nosing in the undergrowth.
We came to believe in her pranks,
even from her point of view: thanks,
says Zuzu, taking her frisbee over the lip
of a cliff, only to circle back and gather in

her scattered pack. You see that?
Not that we've stayed together since.
The day of the possible accident
she chooses a bend in the road
for her disappearing act. We count up to six
lethal vehicles until the sickening squeal
of wheels shoots her back into view.
But by evening she's stiff, her tail twisted,

and the traffic between us is: if can happen. It didn't,
did it? Zuzu's tale is different. In her version,
far from vanishing, I am simply circling
farther and farther away from her.
One lovely grassy day in the summer
I'm to come loping back, enthusiastic,
with news of the living, and say to them
in the nick of time, Missed me. Did you?

Worry Dolls

You can't help yourself. But whatever you'd feared
disappears

into allegory when you open it:
Dr. Caligari's cabinet

of fallen totems. Taken all in all, they are still
far too small to fill in

for the host of problems that have troubled them
into doubles

of us. I mean the ambivalent and unfinished air
their absent stare

can't cover for, and not the oval lip and mouth, mistaken
for a misshapen

lover's oh of recognition. At the least they are a feat
of improvisation. The exposed-wire feet,

bent up from where the kneecaps
should be, and body wrapped

in bandage fabric. Fabulous sandpaper hair. Scattered limbs,
arms akimbo

or straight out, outlandish as a somnambulist's.
The string at the wrists

who can resist tugging at? In their crèche, they're a fetish
which works like this: a wish

whispered to each, pillbox ingredient,
and like obedient

children
or pilgrims

to some makeshift destination, they are off in
their little coffin-

shaped ship too easily to respect them. Eyes mystical;
mouth like Mr. Bill's

dotted on afterthought. They must sleep or else
keep to themselves

during the journey – when you lie awake, eyes wide open
as the ceiling, pried open,

opens onto a face, and a voice smooth as a soothsayer's
utters a prayer

that names your neighbours: Fear of Intimacy. Death.
That's okay, except

from the look on their faces, you know you've been made
in his image and laid

back in your fever bed with a grimace. Now, the nightmare –
was it being speaker, spoken, both or neither?

Nostalgia

After the auction, you brought it all back
home. The unsold odds and ends you now had found
new value in. A broken gramophone, worn down
spelling blocks you'd cut the language on. And your two-story
wooden doll's house, its corners gnawed, stuffed with sawdust
you shook out, evicting its model tenants. A potted annual
past flowering. A comforter you'd sprawled over, bawling
at the sharp thwap of a leather strap. An album, a soother.

The last time you climbed their stairs, the oak bannister groaned
the very sound you heard when you leaned down hard. Thank God
you'd got what you did. The split level you live in
seems more stable – except here's sawdust by the wall
behind the little wooden home your daughter's turning from
to cut out some paper dolls for you, one after one after one.

Personal Effects, Bond's Auction, Woodstock, Good Friday

Everything between the high boy and the baby grand
I'm looking over, with those here after services –
the curious and serious both, come to listen
or lining up to touch the surfaces.

Here's a cigar store wooden Indian, an art deco
figure of a woman, and – good God, why the crowd
around a pair of those baby angels? – unless an
actual's appeared. But the auctioneer's echo

suggests there's no action here, and eyebrows
go up when the baby grand (someone's effects
described now by "lots of age") goes for less than
a grand. I tell myself today I browse,

biding time, though I'm spending it with my ex,
who, bidding with her husband, has been
surprisingly deft. Why am I at a loss when
prices keep rising? Do I envy them

the costs? None of us knows yet that she's expecting.
Watching me lost in pen and paper, would any guess
these lines are my baby of sorts? – "to want less and
less, then, is to know whatever's left

by what has left it, to expect more
from others' spectacles, and to confess
an utter restlessness." And so my lesson
endeth. It's hardly enough, of course,

and I still want what won't be enough, as source
or force – churches, possessions. Whatever
purchase on this world lessens
my searching for more.

Seasonals

Freeze, and over the whole breadth
of the acreage, that awakening
ache in our lungs. The sun and its
godforsaken sundogs
triple and glisten. Sunglasses
prism a thousand odd
needles on the windshield.
Stubble in the fields
makes crystal fists.
Even escaping breath
ices the edifice.
Last night we sat listening
as it whispered in. It was everything
we might have said of it,
seed, rain, tears,
the returning years,
and it was clear
what we needed
instead of it.

Biography Of The Life Between Lives

Captive in stalled traffic
and glimpsing faces on a bus
away from home; the romantic
hints and remnants instilled in us
by vacant places; cloud-drift; snatches
of common songs heard after years;
or odd long moments at dusk
of oblong shadows closing in
on the clearing –
when we shuck off the husk
and let out the dream stuff

drawn through us by the dawn,
this is how God chooses
to touch us,
we imagine,
passing over
the usual attachments.

So, fields of stubble, dust, and chaff
foreign under November snow
more than the feeling of well-being
or even the troubled face of a beloved
I saw – waking in the a.m. again
and hearing the distant chuff
when the furnace turning on
its perfect blue flame
echoed in the flue above it –
naked in bed and shaking
it off, saying enough!

Then feeling it had been enough
until it dawned –
in an inbetween life
is this also a belief
honed when we want
to be left alone?

Aftermath

Of that other rose, grown grand when
the petals, blown and settled together,
resemble a rose, there's so little known
or remembered. And whatever happens
after your love drifts off, whether
on a breath or draft of air, let alone
where it makes its home, I've yet
to gather. But the life it takes on
was your own. And that goes quiet
as a thought or rises from the throat,
aching like the word, when it rose
and turned inward. The high note
unheard where those choir rows
of birds bow a wire. Unspeakable cupids
with beaks for arrows. Kid angels
at bay above a humid, harrowed field.
And, far from eros or harm's ways, muted,
we wait with arms out, the stranger
scarecrows of our feeling days.

The Break

The silence heard
after words

afterwards
grew quieter.

Hyacinth

As though since we've been forgiven
for failing to live in the world,

we can see instead how foreign, unfurled
and naked with its odd-shaped leaf, it

seems this instant – instilled with secret
Grecian marks of god and grief, the sacred

myth it must be hard to bear,
when we bear ourselves away with it.

Afterlife

The Careful Mourner

As if to admonish
anyone lost in
the occasion's demands

for ostentation, the Amish-
lean lines of this coffin,
austere in its brand

of show, astonish
those who've moved off in
that lush satin land

lipping its clamshell. A fond wish,
this wanting something to soften
an awful truth? He can understand

needing to run a hand along this honest
plain grain, as often
must be done. As tears unplanned

complete the feeling that the finish
is coming off on
his hands.

Altered

Dad's been doing better, lately,
eight years on and counting. Mom
had seen him soon after,
sitting in the wingback, and asked
if things were any easier now.
He'd held his face in his hands,
whispered *no* and vanished. However,
on the anniversary, he's come to her
robed in the usual white
light she recalls as tinged with blue,
to say a casual hello. My mother
in her comforter,
nearing eighty years of age...

I miss his face – I do – and can't hear him
or that liquid English accent anymore
in the voices of others. And, lately, Mom,
for reasons I can't fathom,
has been throwing out her photos.
It seems the worry is over
what, if anything, I'll have left
except the loss itself,
a memory of a memory.
  Already now
I'm wondering if I really knew you
well enough. Did I ever see you,
for some idea of you?

The Ghosts

Though I knew about the ghosts
because you told me so, and saw,
after you had vanished, both
the gentleman with the top hat
that passed through the rafters,
and the boy who'd lived before us
in the house, who died in traffic –
you never truly came back
except in dreams. In the last,
you wait for a morning bus
with your hands behind your back
pushing the shoulders forward
in your war uniform, and wear
that banded hat whole decades
after the fashion has passed.
Older than all the other dads
and soldiering on, I understand
in the dream, but not how I'm drawn
through the window, close enough
to your clouding face to touch
or say goodbye. And why,
even knowing it's only a dream,
are my arms passing through?

Diagnosis

In the dream I can tell that you already have it,
there in the softening mouth, the way
your eyes hedge, but habit
is still enough to get you through a day
blue as your ill-fitting sweater.
I also know that there will be no cure.
I'm the one who's getting better.
Nothing if not kinder, patient – I'd say
insufferably resigned to it,
as you were.

Last Words, Already Written

Composed after you had gone
so deeply into your body
our morning had begun,

and before the doctor's awkward smile
stopped at your eyes, bluegreen
islands as blind as eyelids, while

she touched them to shut them.
Before the needle on the dial
neared zero, and we'd been instructed

that the hearing would be last to go,
and before going home, past
Waiting, Admissions, to wake to the phone...

I sat at a desk to rescue them
and asked at last
who I was being, trying to rest you then,

in peace or denial, to find the final
terms of farewell
so soon before the funeral –

knowing the suitable
words would only be found
broken, mutable...

spoken bending over you
as close as we could,
for the good that would do –

when, pen in hand, it happened
again, my being saddened
enough to apprehend

the sad ends
I had put words to.
And if I said then

what I suddenly had to,
hovering above them – *dad,*
we love you – out of the blue

I turned my words over to
see if you'll
seem beautiful

whether or not they're true.

Raised in Winnipeg, Manitoba, Brian Wickers now lives in Toronto, where he teaches English at a private school. His poetry has appeared widely in Canadian publications, including Descant, Fiddlehead, and The Malahat Review, and in the United States in The Atlantic Monthly, Poetry, and The Paris Review. He has held grants from the Ontario, Manitoba, and Canada Arts Councils. Other accolades include being a finalist in the National Magazine Awards (1999) for work published in BorderCrossings, being shortlisted in the "Discovery/The Nation" contest, and winning the 2004 Toronto Star poetry contest.